MW00917272

SUE WOODS

Fun Things to do in St. Louis

A Budget Friendly Guide from a Local

Copyright © 2023 by Sue Woods

All rights reserved. No part of this publication may be reproduced, stored or transmitted in any form or by any means, electronic, mechanical, photocopying, recording, scanning, or otherwise without written permission from the publisher. It is illegal to copy this book, post it to a website, or distribute it by any other means without permission.

Sue Woods asserts the moral right to be identified as the author of this work.

Sue Woods has no responsibility for the persistence or accuracy of URLs for external or third-party Internet Websites referred to in this publication and does not guarantee that any content on such Websites is, or will remain, accurate or appropriate.

Designations used by companies to distinguish their products are often claimed as trademarks. All brand names and product names used in this book and on its cover are trade names, service marks, trademarks and registered trademarks of their respective owners. The publishers and the book are not associated with any product or vendor mentioned in this book. None of the companies referenced within the book have endorsed the book.

First edition

This book was professionally typeset on Reedsy.
Find out more at reedsy.com

Contents

I

Part One

1

Introduction

Welcome to Fun Things to do in St. Louis! My name is Sue Woods and I'm extremely excited to be writing this book! My family moved to the St. Louis area in 1969 and I have called St. Louis home ever since. Raising two daughters here, and now having a grandson, I love all the wonderful things there are to do in St. Louis.

Raising my girls as a single mother, I know what it's like to want to do Fun Things but not have the money to do them. I also know what it's like to visit a new place on vacation and worry that you will not have the necessary funds to have a great time. For those reasons, I wanted to share what I've learned over the years about some very fun things to do that don't take a chunk out of your bank account. Whether you are looking for a Family Vacation or a great place for a Bachelorette Party, there are some great options here in St. Louis.

This book is more of a guide than a book. It won't list all the great things to do in this city, but it will give you some insight on fun things to do that are easy on your wallet. I've tried to make this a book you can refer to when visiting the St. Louis area and make sure you have a great time and stay on budget!

2

Planning Your Trip - The Weather and What to Pack

H ere in the Midwest, we enjoy all 4 seasons. Therefore, packing can be very dependent on the current weather. Missouri writer Mark Twain once famously said, "If you don't like the weather in New England, just wait a few minutes." These words could also easily refer to St. Louis, Missouri, where it's possible to experience several types of weather in just one day. Better to be prepared and bring a few things that you might consider "out of season". Take it from me!

Spring - typically brings mild temps. Although it's not uncommon to see several days in a row with rain or storms.The rain brings with it the blooming of plants and flowers, making a beautiful backdrop to your visit. Temps can vary quite a bit in the spring.

What to pack: You'll want to bring an umbrella or rain jacket for sure. You'll also want to bring clothing that can be layered. Make sure to pack some short and long sleeve shirts, at least one pair of shorts and pair of long pants as well. The evenings will be cooler than the daytime temps, so bring a light jacket.

Summer - Our hottest months are July and August, with temps reaching the high 80's into the 90's. It's not uncommon to have a few days into triple digits. Summers tend to be hot and humid.

What to pack: You'll want to wear clothing that breathes. Shorts and T-shirts are typical summer attire and appropriate for most attractions. Of course, you will want to bring a swim suit for the pool.

Fall – What a gorgeous time of year in St. Louis. The cooler temperatures and crisp air turn the tree's leaves to beautiful tones of red, yellow and orange.

What to pack: Wearing layers in the Fall is always a good idea. You might find yourself wanting to wear a turtleneck sweater at 9am but then by the afternoon, you would rather be wearing a simple long sleeve shirt.Layers are the way to go for Fall! You'll want to bring short sleeve shirts as well as long sleeve shirts. Long pants are a must, but you might want to bring a pair of shorts as well – just in case. A light jacket is a requirement for those cool evenings.

Winter - Our coldest month is typically January with temps in the 30's and 40's. Winters in St. Louis can feel a bit dreary, with most days being cloudy or partly cloudy.The year-round humidity can make it feel chilly and damp. Temperatures are mild but can dip into the single digits when you least expect it.

What to pack: Layers are necessary in winter as well. A turtle neck or scarf for your neck is advisable for those blistering cold days.However, we do get some more mild winter days where all you need is a long sleeve shirt and jeans with a jacket to make yourself comfortable.

3

Traveling to St. Louis and Where to Stay

By *car* - If you're driving to St. Louis, our easy-to-use network of interstate highways makes it a short drive to local attractions. From the east, I-70, I-64 and I-55 head west across the Mississippi River and into downtown St. Louis. I-70 runs north of downtown past the airport and west through Missouri. I-55 turns south past the Anheuser-Busch brewery and continues through southeastern Missouri. I-64, which the locals call Highway 40, continues west through St. Louis, past Forest Park to the Missouri River. I-44 begins in downtown St. Louis and runs southwest along the former path of Route 66 to Springfield, Missouri.

By plane – Our location makes it possible for visitors to fly to St. Louis from most major cities within 3 hours or less. Lambert International Airport is St. Louis' primary airport. There are some smaller airports scattered around the outlying areas as well. MidAmerica St. Louis Airport is in Belleville, IL next to Scott Air Force Base. It is located about 21 miles east of downtown St. Louis and may offer a much more economical rate than Lambert. Allegiant Airlines is the airline to use for this airport.

For smaller private planes, Spirit of St. Louis Airport is in Chesterfield, MO, less than 30 minutes from Lambert. St. Louis Regional Airport is in East Alton, IL, just a short distance outside of the Missouri state line and just 35 minutes from Lambert.

By bus - There are 3 Greyhound bus stations in the metro area if traveling to St. Louis by bus.

By train - There are two Amtrack Stations in the immediate St. Louis region. The downtown station is located at 430 S 15th St, St. Louis, MO 63103. This transportation hub connects Amtrak, Greyhound, and St. Louis' Metrolink and bus services. There is also a station in Kirkwood located at 110 West Argonne Drive, Kirkwood, MO 63122.

WHERE TO STAY

I won't delve into this too much, as the rates for hotels/motels fluctuates tremendously depending on the time of year and what attractions might be holding functions at that time. If there is a Cardinals Baseball game, a Blues Hockey game, or a main event concert in St. Louis, the rates go up, just as they do in any city.

Hotel/Motel - There are many nice hotels and motels located in and out of the city. Because St. Louis has more than 90 municipalities throughout the immediate area, you don't have to stay in Downtown St. Louis to be close to everything there is to do here. Many nearby municipalities are within a 20- or 25-minute drive. You can keep your cost around $100 per night for a hotel stay if you do your homework.

Airbnb or Vrbo - another option if you are on a budget. Here you can find places to rent as low as $40 per night, depending on your needs.

4

Getting around in St. Louis - Transportation Options

The best way to get around in St. Louis is by car or Metrolink. This light rail system offers stops throughout the city and provides easy access to the neighborhoods, attractions, and shopping districts throughout the bi-state region. The Metrolink light rail, has been called one of the best mass transit systems in the country! You can find more information on how to get around using these systems along with maps, schedules, fares and passes on the following link:

https://www.metrostlouis.org/system-maps/

If you don't feel comfortable using public transportation, you can always use Uber or Lyft. Rental cars are another option, but not really budget friendly in my opinion.

Now that you are settled into your accommodations, let's start exploring the City. If you use this guide to plan your activities, I promise you will enjoy your stay and your wallet will thank you!

5

Best Neighborhoods to Explore

The Hill is one of the most popular neighborhoods in St. Louis with all things Italian. Very walkable and tons of great dining options and shops to choose from. Even on a budget, you can find some great options for getting a snack, a meal, or an Italian delight from one of the bakeries.

Soulard is one of the oldest neighborhoods in St. Louis and home to the Soulard Farmers Market, the oldest farmers' market west of the Mississippi River. The area is economically and culturally diverse and located less than two miles from the downtown area.

This area is host to the third largest Mardi Gras Festival in the world. The festivities kick off on January 6 and run through Fat Tuesday with 11 events during that timeframe. The Mardi Gras Grand Parade is the main event. This parade typically includes more than 100 floats, Cajun music, Hurricane drinks and lots of Beads!

You will find live music, and tons of bars and restaurants in this very walkable neighborhood. Plenty to see and do!

The **Central West End** business district is home to more than 75 restaurants, bars and businesses and offers visitors an eclectic neighborhood to explore. There are many annual festivals in this neighborhood. Here, you can also visit the Cathedral Basilica. This spiritual center is home to one of the largest collection of mosaics in the world. There are 49 million glass pieces, and it took nearly 80 years to install. Guided tours are available every day but Saturday. By appointment only.

Forest Park - There is so much to offer inside the park. You'll find the World's Fair Pavilion, the Jewel Box flower conservatory, The Boathouse, two golf courses, Tennis Center, and the Steinberg Skating Rink. Steinberg is the oldest and largest outdoor ice-skating rink in the Midwest.

One of the largest urban parks in the United States, located on 1,300 acres in the center of the St. Louis metro area. Home to the Missouri History Museum, St. Louis Art Museum, St. Louis Science Center, the St. Louis Zoo, and the Muny. Numerous events are held here annually.

The 5.6 mile bike and pedestrian path around the perimeter of the park is enjoyed by visitors and locals alike.

Cherokee Street is located just a seven-minute drive from downtown St. Louis, Cherokee Street has the largest concentration of Latino owned and operated businesses.You'll find a vibrant atmosphere with art, music, and food options very prevalent here. When you see the 20-foot-tall sculpture of an Indian, at the corner of Cherokee and Jefferson, you'll know you are there. Tons of shops, galleries, bakeries, restaurants, and bars can be found in this neighborhood. Love music?You can find everything from hip-hop to jazz to swing music here. Casa Loma Ballroom offers a variety of dance lessons if you're looking to learn a new move or two. Rich in history, Lemp Mansion, Anheuser-Busch brewery complex.

Grand Center Arts District is recognized as the cultural hub of the region, located within a one-mile, 175-acre radius. Offering unique galleries, art museums, performing arts parks, two universities and many restaurants and bars, there is something for everyone. Nearly two million patrons visit annually.

The district hosts more than 1,500 arts and festival events each year. If you like Theatre, you'll want to visit the Fabulous Fox Theatre. Music lover? Enjoy some jazz at Jazz at the Bistro for an intimate performance, dinner and drinks or just a short walk away you will find other genre's of music at the Dark Room, Curtain Call Lounge and more.

Laclede's Landing - Stroll along the riverfront and find dining and entertainment for all.Named after Pierre Laclede who originally surveyed the area in 1763, Laclede's Landing was once a hub for manufacturing, warehousing, and shipping along the Mississippi riverfront. The neigh-borhood features many restaurants and entertainment venues along the cobblestone streets. Annual events such as the Big Muddy Blues Festival are held here as well.

The Delmar Loop or "The Loop" - Located just minutes from downtown, you will find food, music.Home to 140 specialty shops, restaurants, galleries, gift shops and entertainment venues. Home to three live performance spaces including the Blueberry Hill Duck room, Delmar Hall, and the Pageant Concert Hall. See more on those locations below.

Moonrise Hotel – Featuring a rooftop bar and the world's largest revolving man-made moon with painted craters, weighing in at 3,000 pounds and measuring 10 feet in diameter.

Shopping is something you won't want to miss if you like eclectic.You'll find anything from tobacco, tattoos, and tar readings. Don't miss the 70,000 square foot vinyl record store, Vintage Vinyl.

Pin-Up Bowl – Joe Edwards opened Pin-Up Bowl in 2003. This unique and intimate bowling alley stands out with the 1940's pin-up girl memorabilia everywhere. Offering bowling, food, beer, cocktails and more. Games are $4 - $5 game/per person, depending on the day. Parking is FREE.

Maryland Heights is located just 25 minutes from downtown St. Louis, Maryland Heights is full of activities for the entire family to enjoy. See a few of them listed below:

Creve Coeur Park - became the county's first and largest park in 1945 with 2,100 acres. The park offers a 320-acre lake where outdoor enthusiasts can launch their sail boats, rent kayaks or paddleboards, canoe, take a rowing lesson or hike or bike around the six-mile paved Creve Coeur Water Trail, which also connects to the Katy Trail. No swimming allowed. On one side of the park is The Quarry at Crystal Springs Golf Course. On the other side, you will find Creve Coeur Park Soccer Complex with 13 artificial turf fields and seating for up to 500 fans.

Hollywood Casino and Hollywood Casino Amphitheatre – One of St. Louis' most popular outdoor music venues, featuring a superior sound system typically found at sporting events. The venue has a capacity of 20,000 patrons with 7,000 being underneath the roof and an additional 13,000 seating capacity on the lawn.Open from May to October, there is a history of hosting some of the most popular bands and live acts in the world, as well as the most popular festivals.

<u>*Westport Plaza*</u> - is home to several fun things to do:

- <u>*Dave and Busters*</u> - a family-friendly sports bar with hundreds of arcade games.
- <u>*Westport Social*</u> - a classic bar and gaming lounge is also located in Westport Plaza. It features shuffleboard, darts, ping pong, bocce ball, dozens of TV screens, Karaoke rooms and more.
- <u>*Funny Bone Comedy Club*</u> - Looking for a good laugh? Try the local and family-owned Funny Bone. This location has been delivering laughs for over 35 years. Open Mic night every Tuesday at 7:30pm. $5.00 cover and two-drink minimum.
- <u>*Westport Playhouse*</u> - See a variety of Broadway and Off-Broadway entertainment in a small intimate setting at affordable prices.

Chesterfield - Located just 30 minutes from downtown St. Louis, Chesterfield is the largest city in west St. Louis Count. This residential neighborhood was established in 1988 and is home to numerous shopping areas, businesses, arts and culture outlets and much more!

- *St. Louis Premium Outlets* – Located on Chesterfield Airport Rd, this outdoor Mall contains more than 90 designer and name brand outlet stores.
- *The Butterfly House at Faust Park* – Opened in 1998, it is home to over 1,500 free-flying butterflies and 150 tropical plants. Watch a short film about butterflies, view various exhibits or participate in educational programs. General admission is $8.00 for 13+, $5.00 for ages 3-12 and 65+ with children under 2 being FREE.
- *St. Louis Carousel at Faust Park* - The carousel is located in Faust Park and was built in 1921. It features 60 hand-carved colorful wooden horses, 4 deer, and 2 sleighs.
- *Chesterfield Amphitheater* - A beautiful outdoor venue to see your favorite artists! Host to a variety of theatrical, musical, educational, and corporate events with seating up to 4,000 patrons. There is limited parking, with on-site concession and restroom areas.
- *The District of St. Louis* – The District in Chesterfield is a walkable, and unforgettable place where you can eat, play and listen to great music – all in one location. A few things you'll find at the District:

The Hub – This outdoor space provides a great place to gather before heading to some of the other activities in the District.It features a performance stage, pavilion, large LED screen and is located near restaurants and a beer garden.

The Factory – This venue offers 52,000 square-feet specially constructed for live music.The 60-foot-wide stage can be viewed from every seat.

The Main Event – Housed within a 50,000-square-foot space, this family entertainment center features 22 lanes of bowling, laser tag, gravity ropes and hundreds of arcade games to choose from.

Real Dill Pickleball Club – Set to open summer of 2023, it will feature both indoor and outdoor courts, yard games, and a place to get food and drinks.Well suited for competitive players in search of leagues and tournaments, as well as recreational players looking for a friendly game.

Top Golf – A sports entertainment complex that features an inclusive, high-tech golf game that everyone can enjoy. Topgolf provides complimentary clubs or you can bring your own. Order food and drinks or

6

St. Louis Sports – The BEST Sports Fans around

W hen it comes to sports, St. Louis is well known for being one of the greatest Sports towns around. You won't find better fans than those in St. Louis.

Cardinals Baseball - Catch a Cardinals game at Busch Stadium and cheer on our 11-time World Series champions! There are many times during the year that you can get tickets at reduced pricing. Enjoy the game in one of the BEST Sports Towns around! Adjacent to Busch Stadium, you will find Ballpark Village. The 120,000 square-foot multi-story development is visible beyond the left center field all of Busch Stadium, providing a variety of entertainment, food and beverage and on-site parking.

St. Louis Blues Hockey - Part of the Central Division in the Western Conference, the franchise was founded in 1967 and is named after the W.C. Handy song "Saint Louis Blues". The Blues have appeared in the Stanley Cup Finals 4 times, in 1968, 1969, 1970 and 2019, with a Stanley Cup WIN in 2019.

The Blues play their home games at the Enterprise Center in downtown St. Louis.This has been their arena since moving from the St. Louis

Arena in 1994. The old Arena was torn down on February 27, 1999.

St. Louis City Soccer - St. Louis has a rich soccer history. In 2019, St. Louis was awarded an MLS expansion team. 2023 marks the team's first season in their newly constructed soccer-specific stadium in St. Louis City, with a capacity of 22,500 fans.It is located next to Union Station in the city's Downtown West neighborhood.

CITYPARK will host approximately 17-20 regular season games each year. The open-air venue with its canopy roof will also host a variety of community events when not being used for soccer games.

This soccer club is one of the first majority female-owned club in MLS history.

7

The Best Breweries, Distilleries & Wineries to Visit

Anheuser Busch tour – Located just south of St. Louis in the Soulard neighborhood. Tour the Brewery for FREE and learn how Budweiser and other Anheuser Busch products are made.

Everyone 21 and older will receive a free sample at the end of the tour.

Schlafly Beer Tour – Unfortunately, Tours are not available again until the second quarter of 2023. Schlafly Beer opened the first new brewpub since Prohibition in 1991.They have since opened locations in Maplewood, St.

Charles, and Highland, IL. Truly a local company, Schlafly uses only local suppliers for all their products, packaging, and marketing needs.

- Schlafly Tap Room - Opened in 1991, located at 2100 Locust in St. Louis, MO, 63103. Schlafly Bottleworks is located at 7260 Southwest Ave, Maplewood, MO 63143.
- Schlafly Bankside is located at 920 South Main Street St. Charles, MO 63301.
- Schlafly Highland Square is located at 907 Main Street, Highland, IL 62249.

Wineries located in St. Charles County - I urge you to take a drive through the scenic Missouri River Valley. Here, you will find some great wineries located approximately 40 minutes from downtown St. Louis in Augusta and Defiance, Missouri.We call this our very own "Wine Country".

Many of these wineries offer live music on the weekends throughout the spring, summer and fall months. Admission to these wineries is FREE. However, there is a cost to the various wine tastings and food and beverages purchased.

Here's a list of some of my favorites:

Augusta Winery -Located on High Street in August, MO.

Founded in 1980, Augusta Winery offers wine tastings and a wine and beer garden. The tasting room also offers a small gift shop where you can purchase locally produced cheese and sausage to pair with your beverage of choice.

Defiance Ridge – Located on S Hwy 94 in Defiance, MO.

Probably the closest winery as you enter the Defiance and Augusta area, Defiance Ridge sits on 42-acres offering a tranquil lake, lush garden landscape and breathtaking views of the Missouri River Valley. Offering Missouri wines as well as west coast varieties.

Montelle Winery - Located on S Hwy 94 in August, MO.

Founded in 1970, Montelle Winery was the first winery in Missouri with a distillery.Four kinds of brandy are produced here – apple, peach, cherry, and grape. Enjoy some magnificent views while enjoying a glass of wine. The on-site Klondike Café offers some light fare to pair with your wine or brandy. There is also a souvenir shop on-site.

Currently, the Tasting Room is open daily. Sample 4 award-winning wines for $15 or 4 premium/reserve award-winning wines for $20. Receive a souvenir glass with both options.

Mount Pleasant Estates - Located on High Street in Augusta, MO.

Mount Pleasant Estates is Augusta's oldest winery. Originally founded in 1859, the winery was forced to closed when prohibition was enacted in 1920. The wine, all the equipment and vineyards were all destroyed.

The winery reopened in 1966 and sits on 125-acres. The winery grows 9 varieties of grapes offers a 4,000 square-foot tasting room and has some of the most spectacular views around.

Chandler Hill Vineyards - Located on Defiance Rd in Defiance, MO.

The current owners of Chandler Hill began construction in 2007. This winery offers Missouri wines and West Coast wines as well as beer. Tastings are offered and known as the Barrel Room Tasting experience. This lasts between 45 minutes to 1 hour long and can be scheduled on Saturdays between 11 am and 3 pm. The tasting includes 6 wines and small bites. The cost is $45 per person but the fee is waived with a 3-bottle purchase.

Balducci Vineyards - Located on S Highway 94 in Augusta, MO.

Established in 2001, this vineyard covers 76 acres of rolling hills. Also offers a variety of craft beers and food options.

Noboleis Vineyards – Located on Hemsath Road in Augusta, MO.

Established in 2005, this vineyard sits on 84 acres in Augusta, MO. Enjoy a Wine Flight and take in the panoramic views or sample wine in the Tasting Room for a wonderful wine tasting experience.Pizzas and appetizers can be purchased here or you may bring your own picnic basket.

Sugar Creek Winery – Located on Boone Country Lane in Defiance, MO.

Established in 1994, this family-owned winery is located on a lofty river bluff rising from the Katy Trail. It's one of the few wineries that will allow you to bring your own food to enjoy.Wine Tastings are available. They also have beer and cocktails offered for sale.

8

St. Louis Foods You MUST Try & Where to Find Them

Toasted Ravioli – This breaded and deep-fried pasta filled with meat and cheese tops the list of essential St. Louis foods. You can find these on most St. Louis restaurants. Head to "The Hill" for some of the most delicious versions. Charlie Gitto's, Mama's and Zia's are all good options. The Hill is known as St. Louis' famous Italian neighborhood. Hall of Famers, Yogi Berra and Joe Garagiola both grew up on The Hill.

Frozen Custard – This St. Louis staple. The city's most popular place to get frozen custard is Ted Drewes Frozen Custard. With two locations in St. Louis, Ted Drewes has been serving up frozen custard for more than 80 years. You got to try it!

St. Louis Style Pizza – This type of pizza isn't for everyone.You either love it or hate it.It's made with a cracker-thin crust that's cut into squares and mad with Provel cheese, not mozzarella. You can find this style of pizza all over the city, but the best place to is Imo's, which has numerous locations around town.You may have heard their slogan –

"The square beyond compare".

Gooey Butter Cake – Another original to St. Louis, is the gooey butter cake. It was invented when a baker in St. Louis accidentally doubled the butter in his cake receipe. It's essentially a coffee cake with a sweet, custard-like top layer that is served with powdered sugar sprinkled on top. These cakes can be found all over the city, but Gooey Louie is a local shop that specializes in making many varieties of this delectable cake.Missouri Baking Company or Park Avenue Coffee for some of the best.

Barbecued Pork Steaks – This inexpensive cut of meat is a summer must-have. Cooked on a hot grill and heavily sauced, it's usually cooked at home. However, you can also find these on the menu at several St. Louis-area restaurants.

St. Louis Style Ribs – Another BBQ Staple in St. Louis. These pork spare ribs are fattier than baby back ribs and are typically slow-cooked for several hours. Seasoned with dry rub and topped with barbecue sauce as well. Hands down, the best place for St Louis Style Ribs is Pappy's Smokehouse. Another option is Sugarfire Smoke House.

Merb's Bionic Apples – A St. Louis staple for the Fall is this candy-coated apple. These have been served at Merb's for more than 40 years.There are three locations around the St. Louis area. The giant Granny Smith apple is coated in Merb's homemade caramel and then rolled in salted pecan pieces.

Slingers – Perfect for soaking up the booze you drank after a night on the town and fending off a hangover, the slinger is a St. Louis go to. This diner food is typically served in little hole in the wall locations across the city. Most Slingers are made with hash browns, eggs, and a hamburger patty smothered in chili and topped with cheese and chopped onions. For a true slinger experience, you must try the Eat-Rite Diner near Busch Stadium or the Courtesy Diner in south St. Louis.

Fish Fry – St. Louis has a large Catholic population, which means not eating meat on Fridays during Lent. Because of this, many local churches began hosting fish fries on Fridays. St. Cecilia's has one of the best fish fries in town.Lines can be long, especially during Lent, but diners claim it is worth the wait. Another option in Florissant, is St. Ferdinand, offering fish fries year-round.

St. Paul Sandwich – Invented in St. Louis, you will find this sandwich on nearly every Chinese restaurant in the St. Louis area. The original version features a fried egg foo young patty, iceberg lettuce, sliced tomatoes and pickles between two slices of white bread slathered in mayonnaise. For the best St. Paul sandwich, head to Mai Lee's or Old St. Louis Chop Suey or The Rice House.

Gerber Sandwich – This St. Louis original was invented at Ruma's Deli in the early 1970's. This sandwich is made by transforming fresh bread into cheesy garlic bread and then topping with sliced ham, Provel cheese and a sprinkling of paprika before tasting it again. Ruma's Deli now holds a trademark on the name.

9

Arts, Culture and History - Something for Everyone

T   **he Fabulous Fox Theatre** - Located at 527 N. Grand Blvd., this performing arts center is a former movie palace.Situated in the arts district of the Grand Center area in Midtown St. Louis. The Fox Theatre initially opened in 1929 and closed in 1978 after many years of people passing through the brass doors of the Fox to see Broadway shows, Vegas performers, top pop, rock and comedy concert acts, and classic movies.The Fox was re-opened in 1982 and today, the Fox proudly presents something for everyone with over 200 performances and special events taking place annually.

Missouri History Museum - Located in Forest Park at 5700 Lindell Blvd, the museum showcases Missouri history. Admission is FREE but there may be a small fee for special exhibits.

St. Louis Art Museum - Sits atop the hill at Forest Park, located at 1 Fine Arts Drive. It is the perfect place for travelers looking for modern art from around the world. Offering free interactive tours and art-making programs for community groups and organizations.

St. Louis Walk of Fame – Built in 1988 in University City, the attraction contains more than 80 brass and bronze stars celebrating people who were born in or lived in St. Louis and made an impact on the city's cultural heritage.The walk is open year-round and is FREE to the public.

Laumeier Sculpture Park - This outdoor art museum is located in South St. Louis County. There are dozens of pieces of art spread over the 105 acres. Visit for FREE.

City Museum - Located in a former shoe-manufacturing warehouse, this more than 600,000 sq. ft transformed warehouse is fit for all ages. This multi-level playground is filled with caves, slides and climbing apparatuses made from recycled and found objects. Artifacts from all over the world can be found here. Single-day tickets are currently $20 plus tax with children under 3 being FREE.

Missouri Botanical Garden - Founded in 1859 by Henry Shaw. This National Historic Landmark is considered one of the top three botanical gardens in the world. Enjoy the beauty of nature featured in the 79 acres of horticultural displays, including a 14-acre Japanese strolling garden and one of the largest collections of rare and endangered orchids. At this writing, tickets are $14.00 for age 13+ and FREE for ages 0-12. Discounted rates available for St. Louis residents.

10

FREE Things to do for the Budget Conscious Traveler

Purina Farms - Located on more than 300 acres outside of St. Louis, just 10 minutes west of Six Flags, you'll want to bring the kids here. Open from mid-April to mid-October, 9:30am to

3:30pm Wednesday – Sunday. Admission and parking is FREE.

There is an Incredible Dog Arena where spectators can watch dogs of many different breeds perform in an agility course, catch a flying disc, or dive into a 50-foot heated pool. The Purina Farms trainers are available to answer questions from the crowd.

There is a Barn and Play Area for domestic animals typically found on a working farm. Here, children and adults alike can interact with these animals A petting ring in the Barn's nursery area is a favorite for kids. They can interact with piglets, chicks, and baby rabbits. There is also a great Petting Zoo, cow-milking demonstrations and a great play area for the kids.

The Purina Event Center is where a variety of shows take place. These include dog and cat shows where breeders compete for "Best in Show".If you're a cat lover, you'll want to visit the three story cat house.

Grants Farm - This 281-acre farm housing more than 900 animals opened to the public in 1954. Take a tram ride through the park and you'll see lots of free-roaming animals. The tram will drop you off at the Tiergarten, where you can feed a variety of animals. Have your picture taken with one of the world-famous Budweiser Clydesdales at the Bauernhof stables or visit them at their barn located in the guest parking lot. Enjoy a FREE beer sample, courtesy of Anheuser-Busch or have lunch at the Brat Haus or ride the carousel. Please note that although admission to Grant's Farm is FREE, there is a small fee for parking, feeding the animals and the carousel ride.

St. Louis Zoo - Located in Forest Park, hours for the zoo change by season. Please check their website for current hours. Admission to the Zoo is FREE, but there is a $15 charge for parking. Also, some attractions, like the Children's Zoo and the Zoo line Railway do have a small fee. The St. Louis Zoo is home to more than 17,000 wild animals and was first born in the early 1900's. Since the 1970's the zoo has continued to grow and change, with some of the animal stars and Zoo staff garnering worldwide acclaim.

Science Center - Admission is FREE with a variety of things to do with no cost. However, there is a cost for admission to special exhibits and the OMNIMAX Theatre movies and the McDonnell Planetarium shows. Parking can vary from $12 - $15 dollars. Explore the Science Center's 700 interactive experiences, exhibits and attractions.

St. Louis Arch and Museum of Westward Expansion - The arch stands 630 feet above the Mississippi River and is the most iconic landmark in the city. It was built to commemorate the journey westward of colonial settlers through the city of St. Louis, coining the phrase "Gateway to the West". The arch was completed in 1965, with the internal tram system taking visitors to the top and the Visitor Center, opened to the public in 1967.

A decade later, the Museum of Westward Expansion opened underneath the arch. Explore the on-site museum located under the Arch while there, which is FREE. If you want to take a ride to the top of the Arch with the finest views of the City, the cost is between $11-$15 dollars, depending on your age. There are other things to do that can be purchased together. Currently, purchasing a combo ticket including a Tram Ride to the Top, Documentary Movie & One-Hour St. Louis Riverfront Cruise is between $26 and $41, depending on age.

Cahokia Mounds - Located east of St. Louis in Collinsville, IL, this archeological site was once home to the most advanced civilization north of Mexico. You can climb to the top of the Mounds, take a guided tour, or view the exhibits. Admission is FREE but a donation is encouraged.Tours are by reservation only.

World Bird Sanctuary

Get educated on the most threatened species of birds and get an up-close look at bald eagles, owls, falcons, vultures, and more. Located in Valley Park, just southwest of St. Louis, admission and parking are FREE.

Missouri History Museum - located in Forest Park at 5700 Lindell Blvd, the museum showcases Missouri history. Admission is FREE but there may be a small fee for special exhibits.

St. Louis Walk of Fame – Built in 1988 in University City, the attraction contains more than 80 brass and bronze stars celebrating people who were born in or lived in St. Louis and made an impact on the city's cultural heritage.The walk is open year-round and is FREE to the public.

Laumeier Sculpture Park - This outdoor art museum is located in South St. Louis County. There are dozens of pieces of art spread over the 105 acres. Visit for FREE.

11

More Things to Do - These do have a Fee

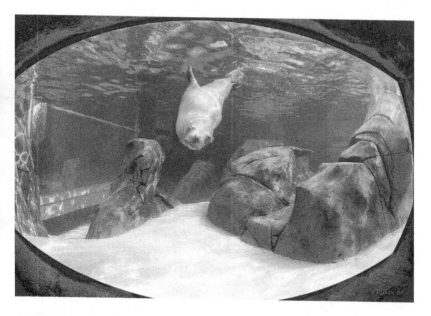

St. Louis Aquarium at Union Station Hotel - Features a 250,000 gallon shark tank, more than 13,000 animals, representing more than 257 species and 44 exhibits. General admission tickets include access to all the galleries, exhibits and interactive experiences.

Advance purchase of tickets is strongly recommended. Cost of admission is $18 for Children age 3-12 and $25 for adults.

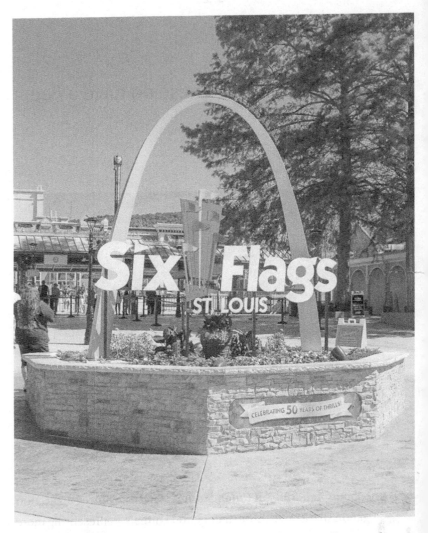

Six Flags of St. Louis - Located in Eureka, MO, just 30 miles southwest of downtown St. Louis. Fun for the entire family! See live shows and concerts, enjoy some fun in the sun at Hurricane Harbor Water Park, or meet your favorite cartoon characters. Currently, Season Passes can be purchased for as little as $59.99 and includes parking.

Magic House - Located in Kirkwood, MO in St. Louis County. The Magic House is an interactive Children's museum where children of all ages learn about science, history, and the world around them. It features hundreds of interactive exhibits where kids can discover new interests, passions, and enjoy a variety of hands-on educational experiences. General admission is $14.00 for adults and children, 1 and up. Or just $3.00 daily after 3pm. Parking is FREE.

12

Outdoor Hiking and Biking

The *Katy Trail* – For Biking or Hiking - The total distance of the Katy Trail in Missouri is 240 miles, beginning in Clinton, MO and ending in Machens, MO. However, locally, the distance between the trailhead in St. Charles and the trailhead in Augusta is 26.8 miles. The trail is known for being flat and smooth.

The trailhead in St. Charles is probably the largest and most developed along the route. Sitting between the Missouri River and historic old town St. Charles, which is full of shops, dining and one of the first micro-breweries in the state – The Trailhead Brewery. Another trail-head frequented often is Augusta, offering many options for wine and breweries in Wine Country. Some of these are located on the Katy Trail itself. If you need to rent a bike, there are numerous options along the trail.

Castlewood Park - for hiking or mountain biking trails – Established in 1974, the park is considered one of the best mountain biking locations throughout the St. Louis area. It straddles both sides of the Meramec River and stretches nearly 5 miles.The park features several picnic sites and a playground, making it a perfect Family spot. There are marked trails for those who want to enjoy mountain biking, horseback riding, fishing, hiking and more. Trails range from 1.7 miles to just under 5 miles.

13

Conclusion

There you have it! All my recommendations for what to do in St. Louis on a budget! I hope it has helped you enjoy a wonderful trip to the wonderful City of St. Louis and not drain your bank account doing it.

If you found this book helpful, I'd be very appreciative if you left a favorable review for the book on Amazon!

Made in the USA
Monee, IL
11 October 2024

67657837R00036